The Journey of the Soul -
The Path of a Medicine Person

Granddaughter Crow

The Journey of the Soul -

The Path of a Medicine Person

Published by
Major Publishing
A division of Major Consulting, LLC
Northglenn, CO

ISBN- 978-1-7329491-0-2

www.granddaughtercrow.com

This book is dedicated to the tribe of the human race. May you be inspired, empowered and discover the passion of your soul as you walk along your soul path.

Half of the proceeds of this book will be donated to The Eagle Heart Foundation.

The Eagle Heart Foundation is a 501(c)(3) nonprofit organization dedicated to charitable giving and educational enhancement.

www.eagleheartfoundation.com

Blessings to All, Granddaughter Crow

Table of Contents

Forward

I first met Dr. Joy "Granddaughter Crow" Gray in 2013, and immediately knew that I was in the presence of someone who carried great power, wisdom, and medicine. It is therefore quite appropriate many years later that she is now sharing that medicine with the world, in her teachings, in her life's work, and now in this treasure of a book.

In the following pages, Granddaughter Crow delightfully shares that medicine people have been recognized as those who carry the sacred wisdom within all things. Each person on Earth, going through certain life initiations, gains and adds to their own unique medicine. That medicine is then, with a deliberate choice on the part of the initiate, available to be given from a loving heart in Divine service to humanity.

Another way to describe a traditional medicine person is to be a walker between worlds. The medicine person has a gift of seeing energy, maneuvering with energy, and perceiving energy that normally is outside the realms of three-dimensional existence. It is a sacred responsibility to be able to travel into those other dimensions of energy and bring the knowledge and wisdom back to Earth for the benefit of the people.

Whether you identify with the role of traditional medicine person or not, it is my belief that we each carry our own unique medicine which, in much the same vein as the traditional medicine person, can be shared with the world at large. Whether you use your gifts and medicine to influence one person or a thousand is up to you. There is no mandate from God as to how exactly to use your medicine, only that you are willing to give it an expression for the benefit of others in your lifetime.

In the following pages, Granddaughter Crow will share with you how you can harness the power of plants and animals and unseen spirits to improve your life and add a depth and richness. Follow along as she guides you through the unseen worlds, navigating you into new realms and dimensions of existence that perhaps you had not previously encountered. With Granddaughter Crow as your compass and guide, you'll learn about the medicine wheel, the elements, the chakras, shamanism, and the seasons and cycles of life that guide and influence our lives, among many other topics.

Prepare to be enthralled, entertained, and informed from the heart of a true medicine woman who I have the privilege of calling my friend. May you be blessed in all your endeavors.

Michael Smith, Ph.D.

Prologue

On Self-Knowledge - Kahlil Gibran

Your hearts know in silence the secrets
of the days and the nights.
But your ears thirst for the sound
of your heart's knowledge.
You would know in words that which
you have always known in thought.
You would touch with your fingers
the naked body of your dreams.

And it is well you should.
The hidden well-spring of your soul must needs rise
and run murmuring to the sea;
And the treasure of your infinite depths
would be revealed to your eyes.
But let there be no scales to weigh your unknown treasure;
And seek not the depths of your knowledge
with staff or sounding line.
For self is a sea boundless and measureless.

Say not, "I have found the truth," but rather,
"I have found a truth."
Say not, "I have found the path of the soul."
Say rather, "I have met the soul walking upon my path."
For the soul walks upon all paths.
The soul walks not upon a line,
neither does it grow like a reed.
The soul unfolds itself like a lotus of countless petals.

Introduction

We earn the medicine that we carry. We earn the wisdom. We earn the rite of passage. We earn these things and more through life's initiations - the difficult times, the dark night of the soul, the hard times that we don't always like to speak about with others.

These Initiations can be sought out; and/or, life will simply present them to us. For me, these difficult periods within a person's life is what gives this individual their medicine (wisdom).

I am a medicine woman, not because of manmade formal education. I am a medicine woman because of the initiations that life has brought to me. Initiations challenge us to grow and to develop. The key is to move through these initiations with balance intact, as much as possible, and to extract the great wisdom that only these times will teach us.

Please join me on the journey of the soul. Let's make it an adventure.

I. The Journey

The Path & Compass

What is *the path*? A path can be defined as a way, or trail, a passageway laid out before us to provide us a route to follow which moves us on a journey and finally to a destination. There are many paths, as many paths as there are individuals. Each individual's path is unique to their soul and their soul's rite of passage. So, how is one to know their authentic soul path? And once you find it, what can act as our compass to guide us? Let's take a step back as we define these things.

There is a school of that we have four bodies of existence: 1) the physical body, 2) the emotional body, 3) the mental body; and, 4) the spiritual body. These four bodies combined will make up an individual. Although there may be more bodies of existence, we will work with this model of four bodies as a starting point.

The physical body is tangible and solid – like the earth. It holds a physical age, a certain physical maturity. The physical body is a part of nature (earth), just like the trees - it is strong, balancing, and in continuous state of self-healing themselves and balancing. Our physical body needs nourishment, rest and exercise to remain healthy and fit. The nourishment that we feed our physical body is physical food. In order to rest the physical body, we can relax, and/or sleep. The exercise that we do to keep it fit and strong requires physical exertion.

While our physical bodies correspond to the strength of the earth, our emotional bodies are fluid and flow like water. It holds an emotional age; however, the emotional age is not necessarily in direct correlation to the physical age. Emotionally, I can feel four years old in one moment and 40 years old in another moment depending on what I am emotionally encountering. Have you ever encountered an individual who is 50 years old physically, yet emotionally responds as a five-year-old in certain situations? Moreover, have you ever encountered a 10-year-old physically, who holds the maturity of an elder? Emotions move like water - they can be refreshing as they ebb and flow. They can come in waves, moving through you and at times overtaking you. They can be stagnant, lacking movement and even sinking into a depressed state. The emotional body needs nourishment, rest, and exercise to remain healthy and fit. The best nourishment we can give our emotional body is positive emotions, such as, understanding, love, grace, peace, and joy, to name a few. The emotional body needs rest (downtime) in order to maintain health. Emotional rest can be found in acts of peacefulness and calmness. There are many ways that we can enter an emotional state of peacefulness and calmness. What works best for you? Emotional exercise can be accomplished with an open heart and connecting with the world around us.

Our physical bodies correspond to the earth. Our emotional bodies flow like water. Our mental body behaves much like the wind – it moves like the air. Thoughts flow in and out, at times they can be as random as a breeze. They can spin like the spiral of a funnel cloud, up and out or spiral into themselves like the eye of a hurricane. They can be calm, as well as, calming.

Our mental body has an age, according to Alfred Binet who published the first intelligence test in 1911. Binet's test was adapted a few years later by Louis Terman, a psychologist at Stanford University – resulting in the IQ test that we know today. The basic concept is the mental age. The revised system measures the intelligence quotient. It measures intelligence with a percentile system. A percentile system that uses 100 points as the average score; hence, approximately 50% of the population will score 100 points on the test. However, only 2% of the population will score over 130 points or under 70 points. Yet, mental age like the ebbs and flows of the air can change depending on an individual and situation. When an individual is tired, hungry, stressed, or simply not feeling well, it will impact his/her mental age. Hence, the mental age can move backward and forwards in its maturity. The mental body needs nourishment, rest and exercise to remain healthy and fit - food for thought. Consider an idea that you haven't had before – this not only feeds the mind, but it exercises it, as well. An individual does not need to adopt every thought that travels through his/her mind. Some thoughts simply need to be recognized and released. It takes a strong mind to entertain a thought that it does not adopt. The ability to hold a thought and focus on that thought takes a healthy mind.

Although mental intelligence is mentioned above, it is worth mentioning that mental intelligence is not the only type of intelligence we have. In 1983, Howard Gardner introduced the theory of multiple intelligence. This theory suggests that traditional psychometric views of intelligence are too limited. Different types of intelligence can be housed in our mental body, physical body, emotional body, and spiritual body, as well. Gardner (2008), outlines his theory suggesting, to date, that there are nine different types of intellect, as follows:

1) Naturalist Intelligence (Nature Smart)
2) Musical Intelligence (Musical Smart)
3) Logical-Mathematical Intelligence (Number/Reasoning Smart)
4) Interpersonal Intelligence (People Smart)
5) Bodily-Kinesthetic Intelligence (Body Smart)
6) Linguistic Intelligence (Word Smart)

7) Intra-personal Intelligence (Self Smart)

8) Spatial Intelligence (Picture Smart)

9) Existential Intelligence (Philosophy and Spiritual Smart, such as, "What is the meaning of Life?")

Flowing from this list, existential intelligence, can touch on and lead us beyond philosophy and towards spirituality. The spiritual body is inspirational - it is like fire. It can purify, keep us energized and inspired. The age of a spiritual body can fluctuate and expand past the physical, emotional and mental bodies, hence the saying, "That person is an old soul." I have found that when an individual begins their personal spiritual path, they may do so for one of two very different reasons. One reason is to grow and develop, the other reason is to escape from reality. Like a baby, the spirit is awakened, it is nurtured and watched over by another. However, at the spiritual age of approximately two years old, the caregivers will begin to show the young spirit how to take care of itself. As the spirit develops more and more, the individual has more and more responsibility to attend to itself and to the world around him/her. If an individual is on the spiritual path in order to escape from reality, the individual usually abandons said path once they are required to assume spiritual responsibility. The nourishment for the spiritual body comes in many forms. There are many spiritual paths; however, one thing is in common with most spiritual paths... the spirit must be nourished.

One way to rest all four bodies at the same time by engaging in the following activity: breathing! The three-fold breath is an exercise that simultaneously benefits our physical, emotional, mental, and spiritual bodies. The first fold is the inhale through the nose, the second fold is to hold the breath within the physical body. The third fold is to exhale and release, again through the nose. Inhaling and exhaling through the nose (vs. the mouth) will activate the parasympathetic nervous system for quicker relaxation. Each of these three folds is given a certain count and cadence that works best for the individual. For example, inhale for four counts, hold for four counts, and exhale for six counts. I encourage every individual to find the count and cadence that works best for them. If one does this exercise for three minutes in the morning and three minutes in the evening, it begins to reset our physical nervous system and relaxes our emotional and mental bodies, as well as, opens up our spiritual body. How? Working with this type of breathing takes us from the beta state into an alpha state. Alpha state is a more relaxed state which impacts all four bodies. Some of the many benefits of increasing alpha state include deep relaxation of the emotional and mental bodies, increased levels of creativity, more focus and improved problem-solving skills, increased the ability to learn something new, and increased serotonin levels. Serotonin is a chemical that directly impacts our mood, contributing to a sense of well-being and happiness, among other medical benefits.

For the reader's edification, here is the basic list of states of consciousness that each of us may enter: 1) Beta, 2) Alpha, 3) Theta, and 4) Delta. As the scientific community continues to research states of consciousness, they may find more than these basic four (such as Gamma state).

1) Beta state is when an individual is fully awake and completely active. In this state, the brain waves operate at a level called Beta where they mainly oscillate between 14 to 30 cycles per second.

2) Alpha state is when an individual's mind is relaxed, and the person enters a more focused, expanded state of awareness where brain wave patterns are mainly composed of Alpha brain waves oscillating at between 8 and 13 cycles per second.

3) Theta state is when an individual relaxes even more, and the mind enters a region that correlates with a large relative quantity of brain wave patterns of 4 to 7 cycles per second. This is the Theta zone of the mind. One can experience profound creativity, characterized by feelings of inspiration and spirituality.

4) Delta state is the level of the mysterious universal mind. It is the level at which the differentiated self (ego) expands to become undifferentiated and operates outside of the confines of linear time/space. In Delta state, the brain waves are less than 4 cycles per second. This is also recognized as deep sleep.

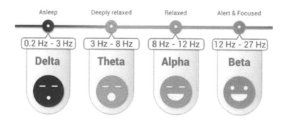

Figure 1. Brain Wave States of Consciousness

Considering that we have four bodies of existence, we can easily recognize that each of these bodies has a maturity level, a need for nourishment, a need for rest, and a need for exercise. However, the physical body is the only one of these four that is subjected and confined to space and linear time (for the most part). The other three bodies can move in and out of space and time with ease. For example, if you were to recall a wonderful memory and sit with it for a moment, you may have a physical, mental, emotional, and/or spiritual reaction as though the wonderful moment is happening in the physical now. Additionally, if you were to visualize a wonderful future and what that would be like, you may have a physical, mental, emotional and/or spiritual sensation as though this is happening in the physical now. Taking time to listen, to feed, to rest, and to exercise each of these four bodies assists us in experiencing a more balanced and harmonious existence.

So how do these bodies work together; moreover, what happens when they are not in alignment with each other? Have you ever physically been in one place, yet your emotions are somewhere else, and your mind is in yet another place, and your spirit is just silent because you're in too many places at one time? I have. I feel lost at these times – like I am not in the right place. Possibly because I am in too many places at one time which can toss anyone out of balance and equilibrium.

So how do we change this? How do we align our four bodies? Here is a model that we can reflect on to assist us in understanding how these four bodies work together. There is a school of thought that the Vitruvian Man by Leonardo da Vinci provides us with a portrait of balance, proportion, alignment, and equilibrium; additionally, one could see the four bodies working together. Although, I do not know the depths of all the meaning that da Vinci portrayed in this masterpiece, and I cannot confirm that he was depicting these four bodies; I can say that this model directly aligns with this school of thought.

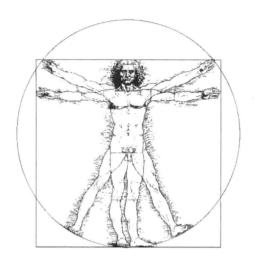

Figure 2. The Vitruvian Man – Leonardo da Vinci

The physical body is depicted by the body standing straight with its legs together and its arms directly outstretched. The emotional body is depicted by the body that appears to be in motion, with the legs spread and the arms reaching higher. The mental body is depicted by the square around the other two, as the mental body can think inside and outside of the box. Finally, the spiritual body is illustrated by the circle which encompasses all the other bodies. This masterpiece provides us with a model which reveals all the bodies working together in balance, proportion, alignment, and equilibrium. All the four bodies in the same place at the same time.

What would it be like if all of the four bodies were in the same place and moving forward in a YES with each other? This sensation is much like love. When I am in love, my physical body desires to be around my beloved. My emotional body wishes to understand what my beloved is feeling. My mental body wants to listen to my beloved's thoughts and perceptions of the world around them. My spiritual body is soaring and dancing with the connection and love between the both of us. When in love the physical, emotional, mental and spiritual bodies are aligned. This is the sensation of being on your path. Love is the path.

I have met my soul walking along its path; when all my four bodies of existence are present. I listen to all my four bodies, giving each of them a voice. This is when I know I am listening and am meeting my soul as it is walking along its path, and I give myself permission to experience the path below my feet on all levels. Hence, the compass is within each of us. It can be experienced in many ways. Some feel it as a vibration of curiosity, some as an internal sense of knowing, some as a sensation of being led. Whichever way this is experienced, the common thread is that one is being directed by the YES, the sensation of being affirmed.

Of course, there is also the sensation of the NO, the sensation of resistance. Without going too deeply into the comparing and contrasting of these two polarities (the YES and the NO), I will say the precise direction is a combination of balancing the YES and readjusting through the NOs. It can be a trade-off betwixt the two in order to accurately direct our will and experience.

At times, we may struggle with figuring out our YES and our NO. Here is a little trick to figuring out the YES from the NO without confusing ourselves by over thinking it. General science reveals that we have approximately 100 billion neurons in our brain. Neurons are nerve cells that receive, processes and transmit information through electrical and chemical signals – our thinking cells, so to speak. Additionally, a human has approximately 40,000 neurons in the heart and an additional 400 to 600 million neurons in their gut. Hence, it is not only the brain that is connecting and thinking, but it is also within the body – kinesthetic intellect. So, one can ask the body for its truth without the brain interfering and potentially overthinking the answer. How? I invite you to stand up with your feet hip-width apart. Next, relax and ground into your feet and lower body without tension or locking your knees. As you sit within your body, make a true statement. If the body agrees with the statement, it will slightly lean forward. Next, make a false statement, if the body disagrees with this statement, it will slightly lean backward. Keep trying until you find your connection.

Keep in mind, if you make a statement and your body leans forward, and backward it is saying that there are truths and falsities within the statement that was made. Hence, simply break down the statement into the truthful parts and extract the non-truth. For example, if I were to say, "I am going to get a new job at ABC company," and my body slightly leans forward, followed by a slight lean backward, I would recognize that half of this statement is true and the other half is not. So, I try it again, "I am going to get a new job," and my body slightly leans forward. Next, I say, "I am going to work at ABC company," and my body leans back. I will recognize that ABC company is not necessarily the company that my body senses that I am going to. Try it with everything, listen to your body – it is speaking with us... just not in words.

A path can be defined as a way, or trail, a passageway laid out before us to provide us a route to follow which moves us on a journey and finally to a destination. There are many paths, as many paths as there are individuals. Each individual's path is unique to their soul and their soul's rite of passage. Love is the path.

I have met my soul walking along its path; when all my four bodies of existence are present. As I move forward in the YES – I recognize that the compass is within me.

Nature & Guides

Medicine people have been recognized as those who carry the sacred wisdom within all things. As you become your own authentic medicine person, take inventory of the rites of passage within your life and extract the wisdom from these experiences. Carry and share this wisdom, live by this wisdom. This is the way of the medicine person. One who connects with the sacred wisdom within all things. For the record, personally, I see all humans as holding the potential of becoming one type of medicine person or another.

A traditional medicine person is tied into the rhythms and forces within nature and animals – within the world around him/her. They hold the ability to see the visible and non-visible world around themselves (Andrews, 2003). They hold the understanding of animism. Animism is a worldview which states that everything has consciousness, moreover, that everything has a soul. Without getting too philosophical about the term soul – I will state that everything has consciousness. All is energy. Energy holds consciousness. I am going to invite you to examine the world around you from this perspective. When one subscribes to the worldview of animism, it may change the way that they interact with the world around them. They may give more respect to the world around them; as well as, become more conscious of the world's rhythm and forces.

23

There are countless spiritual guides that humans can work with along their path on mother earth. I give sacred honor and respect to each of these and all of these. However, much of the time we consider a spiritual guide as an angel, or an ascended master, or an individual who has passed over to the other side, a god or goddess, and otherworldly beings. However, I would like to bring attention to two very profound guides that at times are overlooked – plants and animals. Connection with nature is a powerful guide for us. Nature teaches us the way to live in balance with mother earth. Nature is one of my greatest teachers, and guides.

Plants were here before us, and they will be here after us. According to Buhner (2004), the ancient and indigenous people learned to work with plants from the heart of the world, from the plant itself. They insisted the plants can speak to humans if only humans will listen and respond to them in the proper state of mind. Plants are our teachers and guides.

There are many ways to look at plants as bringers of wisdom. If you are well studied in the plant kingdom, I encourage you to extract all of the metaphors that plants teach us and grow with these lessons. However, if you are like me, you may not know the scientific name for all the plants, but they can still teach us. Each plant has an environmental preference and varying characteristics which make each one unique. Different plants will show us different things.

For example, what if we were to superimpose the plant kingdom onto the human race? What would we discover? We may find that some people are like trees, they grow tall and strong, they provide shade and housing for others. Some people are like rose bushes, they are beautiful to the sight and smell, but the protective thorns might getcha. Some people are like cactus, they are pretty from a distance, but don't hug a cactus.

When we superimpose the plant kingdom onto the human race, we realize that we are not all supposed to be the same, yet we all have a perfect place. The trees are tall and strong. Some of us don't grow as tall, but we are beautiful in our own regard and for our own purpose. We also recognize that at times someone can be our cactus – this is natural, not personal. We also may see why certain people will grow in certain environments, whereas others would not be able to thrive in such an environment.

Plants have taught me many things. One thing is that humans are the only organism on the face of this earth that tries to justify our existence – plants and animals simply don't question who and what they are. Plants will grow into their greatest sense of self – but people limit themselves for one reason or another. I asked the tree, "What gives you the right to be here and to grow so tall and strong? Don't you fear what other plants will say about you?" The tree just waved at me as if to say, "Be more flexible with yourself. Don't compare yourself with others. Simply be the best that you can be." I love plants, they are some of my greatest guides.

Additionally, the spirits of animals are another one of my main guides. The ancestors tell us that animals can come into our lives for a reason, a season or a lifetime. These animals (non-humans) remind us of certain ways of approaching the world around us. Birds, four-leggeds, reptiles and even insects can show us their natural wisdom. Here are some overarching characteristics of these wonderful guides.

A common characteristic of most birds is their ability to rise above the earth and fly. They show us how to do the same. To rise above certain circumstances within our lives and to look at it from a bird's eye view. Many birds were our messengers, such as the carrier pigeons and hawks. Hence, there is an association with birds being our messengers. They also show us a certain type of freedom, which is why we have the saying to not cage a person like a bird.

Just as birds rise above, four-leggeds are grounded and stable as they have all four feet on the ground. Additionally, they will move with one foot in front of the other. This teaches us a grounded step-by-step process and the ability to see what is right in front of us.

Some common features of reptiles and amphibians are that they are cold-blooded – their internal temperature changes with the external environment. Hence, they can aid us in the understanding of how the external realm can impact the internal realm. Many of them will shed their old skin which teaches us to let go of an old self-image and reveal the beauty of the new.

Even insects teach us, some of them teach us the art of teamwork and the strength in numbers. Some of them teach us adaptability, as insects are found in every environment in the world. Some of these will go through grand metamorphosis, and tremendous change, such as the butterfly takes us through her four stages of transformation: 1) egg stage, 2) larva/caterpillar, 3) cocoon/chrysalis, and 4) the adult butterfly or moth.

There are many different guides, I honor and respect them. Yet, let's not overlook the guides within the natural kingdom right here – the plants and the animals. They may not speak English – but they do speak volumes. All we need to do is to pay attention.

Seasons & Cycles

Everything moves through cycles and in seasons. Mankind has recognized this pattern since the beginning of time here on earth. Seasons and cycles are represented historically by the monuments that were constructed around the globe. These monuments were created by laying stones in a particular pattern on the ground-oriented to the four directions. Most medicine wheels follow the basic pattern of having a center of stone(s), and surrounding that is an outer ring of stones with "spokes" (lines of rocks) radiating from the center to the cardinal directions (East, South, West, and North). These stone structures may or may not be called "medicine wheels" by the people whose ancestors built them, but may be called by more specific terms in that nation's language. The art of intentionally erecting massive stone structures as sacred architecture is a well-documented activity of ancient monolithic and megalithic peoples. These cycles, seasonal cycles, hold us globally, as well as culturally.

It embodies the four directions and patterns within life. There are many aspects of the medicine

29

wheel that can assist us in life on mother earth. Although different tribes may interpret the wheel in unique ways, there are some very noticeable aspects that can naturally be recognized by all mankind. The sacred wheel walks us through stages of life, seasons of the year, the elements of nature, and more.

The medicine wheel provides us with the knowledge of the cycles within our individual lives, within our family, within our community, within our participation of mankind as a whole. Traditionally, the medicine wheel has four main sections; however, some ancient cultures will recognize eight sections which align with the seasonal changes of planting and harvest. Below is a short list of what one can find on the medicine wheel.

Direction	Element	Day	Year	Life
East	Air	Morning	Spring	Birth
South	Fire	Noon	Summer	Adolescence
West	Water	Evening	Autumn	Adulthood
North	Earth	Night	Winter	Elder

The system above is widely worked with; however, it is good to note that not all systems will have this same alignment – some tribes will work with other arrangements. However, this is a basic list to reveal the cycles and systems that we live in from a micro to a macro level. Additional elements will be added to this wheel. Animal spirits can be added to each of the four directions. Colors can be added to each. Even manifestation principles can be added.

Here is an example of working with the wheel to manifest something. In the east, come up with an idea or thought. In the south, take action on this thought through research and grounding the idea. In the west, place your emotions into this working and begin to get even more connected with it. Finally, in the north is where the original thought comes manifest. Medicine people will work with the cycles and season to connect with the vital, energetic forces that each cycle and season holds. There are numerous ways to work with the medicine wheel; everything rolls in circles, nature rolls in cycles, and so do we.

The ancestors tell me that we roll through seasons much like mother earth rolls through seasons.

Seasons can be defined as the basic four: 1) spring, 2) summer, 3) autumn, and 4) winter. Or seasons can be defined as a transitional season, a season of rest, a season of joy, a season of mourning, a season of healing, etc. For the purpose of this book, we will look at the four basic seasons.

The springtime is a time to sow seeds and plant a garden – to start something new or renew something old. What shall we grow? Physically, we can grow fruits, nuts, berries, vegetables. Emotionally, we can take on a new practice such as smiling, gratitude, self-care. Mentally, we can sow new ideas that will grow into something wonderful or stimulate the mind to think in different ways. Spiritually, we can start a new practice such as meditation, or learn a new way of spiritually connecting with self and that which is outside of self.

The summer is a time of gaining and growing. Physically, we can grow the plants in the garden we started in the spring. We can tend to it and water it. Emotionally, this may be a time of social engagements and connecting with others. Nurturing these relationships through action and outdoor activities.

Mentally, we can take the new ideas and develop them to prepare for the autumn harvest. Spiritually, it is a time of clarity with the bright sun above bringing light to any darkness to gain and grow in a spiritual practice or concept.

The autumn is a time of harvest and wrapping outside projects up for winter. Physically, we can harvest the plants from our gardens. Emotionally, we may take a relationship to its next level (be it moving forward or releasing it). Mentally, we are able to harvest the manifestation of the idea that we planted in the spring and grew in the summer. Spiritually, this is a time of recognition and realization of how much we have grown and the benefits of the growth we just experienced.

Winter is the time of going within and even a time of hibernation if necessary. Physically, we are drawn indoors where it is warmer, and the days become shorter and the nights become longer. We are able to eat the fruit of our labor throughout the past three seasons. Emotionally, this is the time when we can connect deeper with the more intimate relationships in our lives. When we can pay attention to the desires of our heart, so we know what we would like to plant next spring. Mentally, this is a time to take stock in our thoughts and release the ones that are no longer working for us. Spiritually, it is a time of deeper and more meaningful connection. A time to go within and self-reflect and meditate (although, I do recommend a form of self-reflection and meditation in all seasons). The winter is time to slow down and take notice of what is within.

We roll through seasons much like mother earth rolls through seasons, except that our seasons are not limited to a specific metered time, they ebb and flow as we roll through them. Some personal seasons can last a few days or a few years. Take note of what season you are in and make it the best possible.

Seasons are a type of cycle; however, there are many more types of cycles. A cycle can be defined as a series of events that happen in a specific order and repeats itself. Hence, there is a pattern. From one level, a circumstance may look chaotic, only to find that from a higher level, the same circumstance holds a pattern – even a cycle. Some cycles serve us. Some cycles harm us. It is good to consider the individual and group cycles that we are in, in order to gain a deeper understanding of these cycles. We can then consider if the cycle is working or not. We can then consider if we would like to add something to the cycle, delete something from the cycle, or revamp the cycle completely. Awareness of the cycles is essential if one would like to consciously change the cycle.

Some cycles are seasons, as shown above. Some cycles may be experienced within one day. For example, in the morning I wake up and start my day, Noon is when I eat lunch and reinvigorate. In the evening, I begin to relax and nighttime, I rest – and repeat. We can superimpose the concept of the day into our lifetime.

The Chakra System as a Map

In general shamanism, there are three basic worlds (aka realms). There is the lower world/realm, the middle world/realm, and the upper world/realm. Although the concept of shamanism is worldwide and found in multiple cultures around the globe, the basis is a medicine person who acts as an intercessor between the worlds/realms on behalf of others. Others can be defined as a person, a place, a thing both physical and non-physical. Although there are countless worlds/realms, for this book, we will work with the model of three basic worlds/realms. This will be the map in which we explore.

To go on a journey, one is successful when they have a point of reference, a map. A map assists us in gaining our coordinance – a point of position and reference. To understand the three worlds/realms, I invite you to superimpose the seven primary chakra system as a model in these three realms. As the ancient saying goes, "Know thyself, and you will know the universe." This is a school of thought that allows us to examine and experience the three realms with deeper references, beyond the traditional explanations.

First, we will look at the seven chakras. Then we will bump them up against the three worlds in order to gain more clarity.

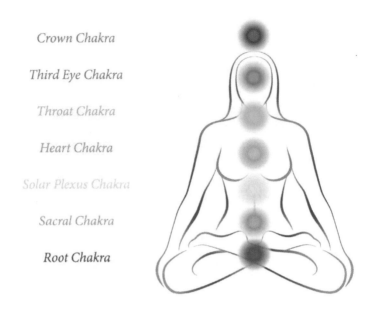

Crown Chakra

Third Eye Chakra

Throat Chakra

Heart Chakra

Solar Plexus Chakra

Sacral Chakra

Root Chakra

Figure 3. The basic seven chakras

Chakras are known as vital energy points of life force. In Sanskrit, the meaning of the word *chakra* is "wheel" or "disk." It is believed that at the inner core of each one of us spins seven wheel-like energy centers called Chakras. Judith (2010) stated, "The chakras are gateways between various dimensions – centers where the activity of one dimension, such as emotions and thought, connects and plays on another dimension, such as our physical bodies" (p. 17).

Each of these chakras reflects an aspect of consciousness which is essential to our lives. Moreover, chakras have three main functions: 1) to receive energy, 2) to assimilate energy, and 3) to transmit energy (Judith, 2010). Together, these seven chakras form a profound formula for wholeness that integrates physical, emotional, mental and spiritual bodies. As a complete system, the chakras provide a map to understand where we are and what we desire and directs us towards where we would like to go.

Chakra One – Root Chakra – Earth

Keywords and Functions: Survival, Grounding, Earth, Roots, Physical Body, Beginning

Sanskrit Name: Muladhara

Sanskrit Meaning: Root Support

Color: Red

Symbols: Four red petals, around a square containing a downward pointing triangle.

Inner State: Stillness, Security, Stability

Foods: Proteins

Rights: Right to be here, Right to have

Corresponding Verb: I have

Some Stones: Agate, Bloodstone, Tigers Eye, Garnet, Ruby, Hematite, Onyx, Smoky Quartz, any red stone

Some Oils: Cedarwood, Patchouli, Myrrh, Musk, Lavender

Chief Operating Force: Gravity

Chakra Two – Sacral Chakra – Water

Keywords and Functions: Emotions, Nurturance, Relations, Desire, Pleasure, Sexuality, Procreation

Sanskrit Name: Svadjostjana

Sanskrit Meaning: Sweetness

Color: Orange

Symbol: Six orange-red petals which contain a second lotus flower and a crescent moon. Within the moon lies a Makara, a fish-tailed alligator with a coiled tail. Connected to the sciatic nerve – hence it can also be called the seat of life.

Inner State: Feelings

Foods: Liquids

Rights: I have the right to connect

Corresponding Verb: I feel

Some Stones: Citrine, Carnelian, Golden Topaz – Gold and Yellow Stones

Some Oils: Jasmine, Rose, Sandalwood

Chief Operating Force: Attraction of opposites

Chakra Three – Solar Plexus Chakra – Fire

Keywords and Functions: Power, Autonomy, Metabolism, Transformation, Self-Esteem, Will, Assertiveness

Sanskrit Name: Manipura

Sanskrit Meaning: Lustrous Gem

Symbol: Ten petal lotus flower containing a downward pointing triangle surrounded by three T-Shape svastikas, or Hindu symbols of fire.

The downward pointing triangle is a symbol for Shakti, sacred divine feminine in Hinduism.

Inner State: Laughter, Joy, Anger

Foods: Starches

Rights: I Am

Corresponding Verb: I Can, because I Am

Some Stones: Yellow Citrine, Sunstone, yellow stones

Some Oils: Rose, Ylang Ylang, Cinnamon, Carnation

Chief Operating Force: Combustion

Chakra Four – Heart Chakra – Love

Keywords and Functions: Love, Balance, Sympathy & Empathy, Unity, Healing.

Sanskrit Name: Anahata

Sanskrit Meaning: Unstruck. Love is "unstruck," and flows most powerfully in a heart that loves fearlessly.

Color: Green

Symbol: Lotus of 12 petals, containing two intersecting circles that make up a 6-pointed star demonstrating the perfect balance between the downward and upward – masculine and feminine. The triangle facing upward symbolizes Shiva, the male principle; while the triangle facing downward symbolizes Shakti, the female principle.

This chakra is the middle chakra, the balancing point of the lower three and the upper three. This is where we are able to connect and balance the higher consciousness with our grounded expression for our greatest potential to become manifest. We are now free to "follow our own heart." This sacred space within our heart is a space where the wisdom of the council solidifies, and if we listen, we can hear the secrets of the universe: a language older than words. This is the wisdom of the heart.

> *Your hearts know in silence*
> *the secrets of the days and the nights.*
> *But your ears thirst for the*
> *sound of your heart's knowledge.*
> *You would know in words that which you have always*
> *known in thought.*
> *You would touch with your fingers*
> *the naked body of your dreams. – Kahlil Gibran*

Inner State: Compassion and Love.

Foods: Veggies

Corresponding Verb and Rights: I Love – I have the right to experience love. To love and be loved.

Some Stones: Rose quartz, Emerald, Green calcite, Jade, Aventurine, all green stones

Some Oils: Rose, Bergamot

Chief Force: Equilibrium

Chakra Five – Throat Chakra – Sound

Keywords and Functions: Sound, Vibration, Communication, Mantras, Song.

Sanskrit Name: Visuddha

Sanskrit Meaning: Purification

Color: Blue or Sky Blue

Symbol: Lotus with 16 petals containing a downward pointing triangle within which is a circle representing the full moon... cosmic sound and is surrounded by lotus petals.

Inner State: Synthesis of ideas into symbols

Foods: Fruits

Corresponding Verb: I Speak

Right: I have the right to share and express

Stones: Turquoise, Lapis Lazuli, Aquamarine, Sodalite, Sapphire, any Blue Stone

Oils: Chamomile, Myrrh, and Ricola.

Chief Force: Commune and Express

Chakra Six – 3rd Eye Chakra – Light

Keywords and Function: Light, Seeing, Intuition, Visualization, Imagination, Clairs, Vision

Sanskrit Name: Ajna

Sanskrit Meaning: To perceive, to command

Color: Indigo

Symbol: Lotus with two petals on either side resembling eyes or wings, around a circle containing a downward pointing triangle. These two petals also represent the manifested and the un-manifested mind and are sometimes said to represent the pineal and pituitary glands.

Inner State: I perceive

Foods: None or Entheogens (altered states of consciousness)

Rights and Corresponding Verb: I See, and I Perceive

Some Stones: Silver, Sapphire, Lapis Lazuli,

Some Oils: Saffron, Acacia, Mugwort

Chief Force: Intuition

Chakra Seven – Crown Chakra – Cosmic Energy

Keywords and Functions: Consciousness, Universal Thought, Information, Knowing, Deep Understanding, Transcendence, Meditation

Sanskrit Name: Sahasrara

Sanskrit Meaning: Thousand Petal Lotus Flower

Color: Violet, Gold, White

Inner State: Bliss

Right and the corresponding verb is: I am one with everything.

Foods: None - Fasting

Some Stones: Diamonds, Amethyst, Clear Quartz, any white stone

Oils: Lavender, Frankincense

Chief Force: One with the All – I am a part of the whole.

These are some of the basic attributes of the seven chakras. In the next three chapters, these chakras will correlate with the three worlds of existence. The breakdown is as follows.

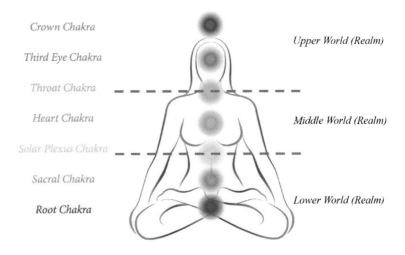

Figure 4. Seven basic chakras and three worlds

The hidden well-spring of your soul must needs rise and
run murmuring to the sea;
And the treasure of your infinite depths
would be revealed to your eyes.
– Kahlil Gibran

II. The Lower World

The lower world can also be described as the underworld. Individuals (medicine people) can drop down into the underworld on behalf of self or others in order to bring harmony to the whole. If there is a blockage or an imbalance within the underworld, it can and will be mirrored in the middle and upper worlds.

In accordance with the chakra system presented at the end of chapter one, the lower world can directly correlate to the lower 2.5 chakras. The root chakra, the sacral chakra and half of the solar plexus chakra.

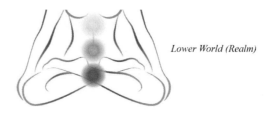

Solar Plexus Chakra

Sacral Chakra

Root Chakra

Lower World (Realm)

In order to understand the lower world, we must revisit the keywords and functions of these chakras. Keeping in mind the three main functions of each chakra are as follows: 1) to receive energy, 2) to assimilate energy, and 3) to transmit energy (Judith, 2010).

The root chakra's keywords and functions are survival, grounding, earth, roots, physical body, beginning, and the corresponding verb is "I have." The right of the root chakra is "I have the right to be here." For example, when the root chakra is blocked an individual may struggle with the sense of not belonging or feeling unstable. If unblocked, the root chakra recognizes the right for self and others to be here as a symbiotic organism.

The sacral chakra's keywords and functions are emotions, nurturance, relations, desire, pleasure, sexuality, procreation, and the corresponding verb is "I feel." The right of the sacral chakra is "I have the right to connect." For example, when the sacral chakra is blocked an individual may struggle with connecting with others and possibly a lack of creative flow. If unblocked, the sacral chakra recognizes the connection between self and others and is empowered to create and/or procreate.

The solar plexus chakra's keywords and functions are power, autonomy, metabolism, transformation, self-esteem, will, assertiveness, and the corresponding verb is "I am." The right of the solar plexus is "I have the right to be who I am." For example, when the solar plexus chakra is blocked an individual may struggle with the sense of self and self-empowerment or the sense of their will and willpower. If unblocked, the solar plexus chakra recognizes a health form of self-empowerment. The rest of the chakras system is visited later in chapter III and IV of this book.

The Landscape

There are many landscapes in the lower world. These landscapes can reflect those within the middle world (the physical world in which we physically exist). However, they are not limited to these landscapes.

For example, in the lower world one may find a landscape that is familiar, such as a jungle, an ocean, a desert, and so forth. Whatever the shapes and sizes of things within the landscape may be disproportionate to that which we will find in the middle world. Not only the physical landscape, but seasonal landscapes are represented in the lower world. It could be spring, summer, autumn or winter. Additionally, it could be morning, noon, evening or night. Each of these elements holds certain meanings, and when weaved together in the conscious energy that the landscape of the underworld is attempting to express, interpretations may vary and can be very specific once understood.

What beings may one encounter in the lower world? There are unlimited forms of energy. However, it is common to find instinctual human and non-human entities within the underworld – beings who are very basic in their instincts. In so much that I directly align the underworld to the reptilian portion of the human brain – the fight, flight and freeze mode, and the hunter and gather aspects. The basic root and sense of

51

belonging, as well as self-awareness. When journeying to the underworld, it is essential to establish allies within the landscape that will be able to work with you. In the next section of this book, there is a guided meditation to the lower world to meet some of these allies if you wish.

The Phenomenon

There are many reasons why someone would want to journey to the lower world (the underworld) – it would be nearly impossible to record all of them here in this book. However, I do want to provide a personal and professional example of what can occur.

One time I was working with an individual in a business setting who was very abrasive. I understand that some people can be naturally abrasive, and that is fine. In this situation, the individual made it clear that they were intentionally abrasive with me because they didn't respect me for one reason or another. Nevertheless, this situation was growing old, and I wanted to effect change.

So, one day, I journey to the lower world and meet this individual in his office (a lower world replica of a middle world office). The lower world replica of his office was very recognizable; however, there were more spider webs in the shadows, and the colors were muted (less life force – less free-flowing air). The temperature in the room was cold, and it made me shiver. I sat down and greeted the lower world version of this man. Needless to say, my lower worldview of this man was UGLY!

I stated who I was and that I have come to see about resolving and rebalancing the situation we shared. I told him what I had learned from our exchanges – such as I learned to listen, yet not take everything personally. I learned that I have the strength to work with an individual who doesn't respect me, and not to take it too personally. I learned to not allow my work to be negatively affected by our exchanges. I told him thank you for the lessons. I asked him if there was anything more that he was sent to teach me. When he said, "No, that's all I can teach you." I responded, "Good. Thank you. I declare our contract over, and I am ready to move on to my next teacher."

With that, his lower world spirit vanished into thin air, and another being showed up in his chair. This being was a female with blonde hair. She smiled at me and said, "Let's get to work." And the lower world journey ended.

The next week when I went to meet with the original man, I was notified that he was transferred to another department and that I would be meeting his replacement today. I was excited to see if it were a woman with blonde hair. When I met her, I was disappointed to see that her hair color wasn't blonde – it was red. Nevertheless, I accepted this new relationship and found her to be a good business partner. A few days after our first meeting, she was still settling into her new office, and she had some family photos on her desk. When I looked at one of the photos, in particular, I had to take a step back. It was her with blonde hair. I asked her, "Is this you?" She told me that it was her twin sister and that the only way people could tell them apart was because she dyed her hair red. She is a natural blonde. Yes!

That day, I learned some important lessons. I learned the impact that traveling to the lower world has on the other worlds. I learned to negotiate with other beings versus showing up to battle. I also learned that dyeing one's hair in the middle world, doesn't seem to transfer to the lower world – talk about not dyeing your roots!

The Hidden Treasures

What are the hidden treasures of the lower world? What is the purpose of exploring this realm? How do I explore this realm?

There are countless reasons why one would travel and explore the lower world, so let's start with what we know thus far from the chakra system. Keywords and functions are survival, grounding, earth, roots, physical body, beginning, and the corresponding verb is "I have." The right of the root chakra is "I have the right to be here." The solar plexus chakra's keywords and functions are emotions, nurturance, relations, desire, pleasure, sexuality, procreation, and the corresponding verb is "I feel." The right of the solar plexus chakra is "I have the right to connect." The solar plexus chakra's keywords and functions are power, autonomy, metabolism, transformation, self-esteem, will, assertiveness, and the corresponding verb is "I am." The right of the solar plexus is "I have the right to be who I am." Think of the lower world like the roots of a tree. The roots provide the foundation, health, connectedness, stability, etc. Hence, these are the aspects that one would find in the lower world. Additionally, an individual would be able to understand these basic aspects within ourselves and others by journeying to the lower world. The basis of life, relations and a sense of belonging.

Examples: I have traveled to the lower world to assist in rebalancing energy to promote healing, to assist with understanding relationship dynamics between people, places and things. I have traveled to the lower world to also learn from my ancestors and my roots.

There are countless situations that one could journey to the lower world for; however, it is essential to state one's intention before embarking on a journey. Additionally, you may want to seek out an individual (Shamanic Practitioner) to assist your journey who will journey with you or journey on your behalf. Safety is key!

This being said, I have created a guided meditation for you that will be safe and easy so that you will be able to experience the lower world in a safe and sacred guided spiritual way. Below you can read about it, and you can also find this guided meditation on the Granddaughter Crow YouTube channel if you'd like to experience it without interruptions. Or find a friend with a calm voice to read this to you (take turns, it's fun).

First, place yourself in a comfortable place that you feel safe and will not be disturbed. Then sit or lay in a relaxing manner. Next, begin to breathe with the three-fold breath that is mentioned earlier in this book. Breathe like this for at least a minute, more if you'd like. Next, do a body scan and check in with your body to see if there is any part of you that would like to shift and/or relax more. Please feel free to relax even more.

If you need to shift your body at any time during this meditation, it will not disturb the meditation at all. Please feel the comfort of this sacred space. Now, let's continue... Visualize that you are in a comfortable sphere. Within this sphere is sacred space, visualize a beautiful, yet peaceful light filling up this sphere with sacred loving energy. Now, as you breathe in, know that you are breathing in sacred energy. As you hold it within your being, know that you are holding sacred energy within your being. As you exhale, know that you are releasing and relaxing into sacred space. We are ready to begin our journey.

We are at the top of five steps. Let's descend these steps together. Five, relax, four, relax, three, relax, two, relax, one. Now we find ourselves in a small yet cozy room where there is a table, a coat rack, and a door. First, let's move over to the table. I invite you to set down anything and everything that you are carrying and place it on this table. There is a sign from the Universe above the table, and it reads, "Anything that you set here, will be taken care of."

Next, let's move over to the coat rack where we can hang up the many hats and cloaks that we wear in our daily lives. Now, prepare yourself, as we are going to move over to the door. Beyond this door is a beautiful land of your profound imaginings. When you are ready, open the door, step through the door, and allow the door to gently close behind you.

You have entered a beautiful land. Let's move into this landscape together. Notice the landscape as it reveals itself to you. Allow it to unfold and settle in. Become aware of what is above, what is below, what is around you.   As you continue to move into this landscape, you notice that you are on a unique path. Let the path lead you through the landscape. Step by step... this land is unfolding to you. The air is alive, breathe it in. Note the time of day or night– the season - as this world becomes more and more alive.

As you continue down your path...become aware of a tree directly in front of you. Take a moment and allow the tree to focus into your sight. If it reveals itself... note what type of a tree it is.

Now approach the tree and find a special place to sit and relax under it. Your back may lean against this tree.   As you make yourself comfortable, take another deep breath and relax into the tree. As you feel the tree touching your back, know that the tree feels you too. You and the tree now have a connection – you are becoming one. As you relax deeper into the tree, you begin to realize that the tree is wrapping itself around you like a warm blanket and drawing you into itself.   Relaxing, even more, the tree invites your consciousness to its roots, the roots are like a rope that invites you down into the ground. Feel the earth around you. Notice what it feels like as you move through it guided by the root rope. Prepare yourself, for in a moment we are going to pop into the underworld. Three, two, one, let go of the root rope and land on the top of a mountain cliff in the underworld. It is safe here... be here for a few moments and notice what is around you as it comes into vision. There are many landscapes in the underworld, many animals, much magic. Begin to breathe in the air.

Now we are here. I will tell you that a Shaman is standing next to you. On the Shaman's left shoulder sits a raven. On the Shaman's right-hand side sits a black jaguar (a panther). These are your allies here on this adventure. They are here to protect you and watch over you here. This Shaman is very powerful and very kind. These allies may join you for the rest of your journey, or simply watch over you from a distance... whatever happens, they are here.

As a greeting, the shaman offers you a drink of tea – it tastes of the earth. As you partake of this tea, you will become refreshed, and your vision and agility in the underworld will become stronger.

Now, notice the lay of the land, and we are going to begin to move into the landscape. Notice what you feel like as you peer across the landscape. Let's begin to move into the landscape. The Shaman takes your hand and moves you into the landscape.

Now, you are standing in the landscape of the underworld. Here there is a powerful animal who has been waiting just for you. Call out to this animal, and he/she will come to you. This animal is your special guide here. Quietly from the voice within, call out to your animal guide. "Come, come, come." Now sit quietly, I hear them coming. You will know which one is yours... your eyes will meet their eyes, or you will sense a great connection. They live here.

As they arrive... spend a few moments with them. Notice their color, any unique aspect about them. Take your time. Allow them to take you on a journey and show you around. They want to take you to a special place here. They have a special gift for you.

Take your time, and I will wait here in silence for you for a few moments. (pause here for at least 3 min in order to connect with the underworld).

61

The Shaman has come and is going to lead you back, but before we go... note this sacred place. For, you are able to return any time that you wish. Follow the Shaman, back to the edge of the cliff. There is a doorway in the cliff that looks like a cave. As you walk through this doorway, it gently closes behind you, and you begin to rise up like an elevator. Up, up, up until you reach this room and step back into the physical space. Take your time...

In your own time, wiggle your fingers and toes, and when you are ready, gently open your eyes. Welcome back from the lower world to the middle world. At this point, I would like to invite you to either write down or discuss with a trusted friend what you encountered. If you encountered an animal, look up the spiritual meaning of that animal. If you encountered a certain landscape, look up the meaning of the landscape. Just like waking from a dream, it is time to sit with the experience and allow the meaning to unfold. What hidden treasure did you find in the lower world?

But let there be no scales to weigh your unknown treasure;
And seek not the depths of your knowledge
with staff or sounding line.
For self is a sea boundless and measureless.
– Kahlil Gibran

III. The Middle World

The middle world is the physical world in which we physically exist. It contains universal law and systems set up by natural law, such as the natural law of cause and effect. Many of these laws are brought to us via physics. Physics reveals natural law to us through observing matter and its motion and behavior throughout space and time. We can extract these natural laws and let them define the motion and behavior of our path throughout space and time.

In accordance with the chakra system presented at the end of chapter one, the middle world can directly correlate to the middle chakras - half of the solar plexus chakra, the heart chakra, and half of the throat chakra.

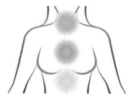

Throat Chakra

Heart Chakra   *Middle World (Realm)*

Solar Plexus Chakra

In order to understand the middle world, we must revisit the keywords and functions of these chakras. Keeping in mind the three main functions of each chakra are as follows: 1) to receive energy, 2) to assimilate energy, and 3) to transmit energy (Judith, 2010).

Again, the solar plexus chakra's keywords and functions are power, autonomy, metabolism, transformation, self-esteem, will, assertiveness, and the corresponding verb is "I am." The right of the solar plexus is "I have the right to be who I am." For example, when the solar plexus chakra is blocked an individual may struggle with the sense of self and self-empowerment or the sense of their will and willpower. If unblocked, the solar plexus chakra recognizes a healthy form of self-empowerment.

The heart chakra's keywords and functions are love, balance, sympathy & empathy, unity, healing, and the corresponding verb and the right of the heart chakra is "I love." For example, when the heart chakra is blocked an individual may struggle with love and compassion of self and others. If unblocked, the heart chakra recognizes the love of self and how to love others in a positive way.

The throat chakra's keywords and functions are sound, vibration, communication, mantras, song and the corresponding verb is "I speak." The right of the throat chakra is "I have the right to share and express." For example, when the throat chakra is blocked an individual may struggle with expressing themselves. If unblocked, the throat chakra is able to express one's truth in an influential manner.

The Landscape

The middle world is the physical world in which we physically exist. Obviously, there are many landscapes in the middle world. Not only natural landscapes but human-made landscapes, as well. For example, a natural landscape would be the mountains, the forest, the ocean, the jungle, and the desert to name a few. However, man-made landscapes would consist of our home environment, work environments, personal and social environments, political environments. Although we may not automatically consider these environments as landscapes, something mysterious happens when we describe our human-made environments metaphorically with natural environments and landscapes.

For example, what if I were to say that my home environment is like a magickal forest; yet my work environment is like a dark swamp. One would be able to extract that I have a wonderful lively home life; however, a stagnant work life that is in need of more fluidity and flow. Working with nature-based metaphors can assist us in understanding the emotional, mental and spiritual landscapes within the middle world.

We are aware and continue to learn the types of beings we will find in the middle world (people, animals, plants, etc.). It is almost awkward to address this in this section. However, it is good to note that there are otherworldly beings in the middle world – both seen and unseen. Sounds like I am talking about ghosts, angels, and demons and maybe I am. However, if we reflect on the concept of animism described in chapter one, we will recall that everything has consciousness (human and non-human alike). If everything has consciousness, seen and unseen, I suggest that there truly is a spirit of happiness, a spirit of death, even a spirit of Christmas.

Moreover, I am talking about all spirits and entities seen and unseen and human and non-human. This opens our minds to consider that the landscape of any world contains another dimension to it – an emotional dimension, a mental dimension, and a spiritual dimension. Hence, I may walk into a toy store in December and encounter the spirit of Christmas. Just like I could walk into a hospice and encounter the spirit of death – even if it is indirectly touching me. Additionally, I could walk into a forest and encounter the spirit of life, peace, and balance.

The Phenomenon

The phenomenon of living in the middle world is ever expansive. Each of us has our own experiences and stories. However, do these phenomenons hold any meaning to us? Sometimes, yes. Sometimes, no. Sometimes we may find ourselves drifting through life on autopilot. Some people will seek a more meaningful relationship, a more meaningful career, a more meaningful life. This is awesome; however, I would like to interject another idea. What if meaning begins within a person versus meaning coming from outside of a person. For example, I could walk past the rose bushes outside of my house and not even take notice. Then one day, I cliché(ingly) stop to smell the roses. That day, the roses have meaning to me although they have always been there.

How can I find the meaning in the life I already have? One way is to engage your five senses: 1) sight, 2) smell, 3) touch, 4) taste, and 5) sound. Abram (1997) states, "Humans are tuned for relationship. The eyes, the skin, the tongue, ears, and nostrils—all are gates where our body receives the nourishment of otherness." (p. ix). When we engage with our five senses, the world becomes more alive to us.

Next, we need to allow the deeper meaning to come from the experience and/or phenomenon. One way to allow the meaning to come is through a process called reflective writing. Reflective writing deepens the understanding and solidifies the meaning of an experience. Setting aside prejudgments of quick interpretation, allowing the text or phenomena to present itself to itself. Moustakas (1994) quotes Nietzsche, "There are no moral phenomena, only moral interpretations of phenomena" (p. 9). This attitude suspends predefined judgment and seeks for a clear perspective of the phenomenon. Reflective writing as described by van Manen (2002) takes in meaning, interpretation and deeper truths.

How does one engage in reflective writing or even reflective thinking or reflective conversations? Reflective writing is to simply sit down with pen and paper or a computer and to start with what you recall from any phenomenon. Next, review what you've recorded and extract any elements that pop out at you. Then, individually look at these elements and see what meaning you place on these, what meaning others place on these and what meaning comes up within you when you consider each element. Record that as well. Finally, read over all that you have recorded thus far and allow for more meaning to emerge – such as a memory or a strong feeling. Now, we are gaining the deeper meaning of our world.

Reflective writing is a helpful tool to extract meaning from any phenomenon. Reflective writing can, also, assist us with dream interpretation. Additionally, it can assist us with interpreting any journeys that one takes to the lower or upper worlds. We live in a world of moments, each moment is a phenomenon. It is up to us to gain the deeper meaning in our world – if we choose to do so.

For example, the phenomenon of stopping to smell the roses that grow outside of my house. I would write about what day and time it was when I noticed them. Possibly a quality about them that I noticed with each of my five senses. I would then write about what a rose means to me personally, what roses mean in general. Next, I would allow for possible memories to emerge. Over 20 years ago, I remembered picking out this particular rose cultivar because of the size, color, and smell. I remember building the planters and how much work I put into them. I remember planting them and watching them grow every year. The years of me raising my son. The years of my going through sickness. The years of me going through school. The years of finding my way and falling in love with my beloved spouse. Then I realize that these roses have watched my life and have witnessed over 20 years of my existence – it's hard to find a friend who will stick around for that long. I realize that these roses hold a significant place in my memory, my heart, and they are right outside my front door. Now, I have found my meaning within the roses and deeper meaning within my life.

The Hidden Treasures

What are the hidden treasures of the middle world? The middle world is where our physical body exists; hence, it is here where we are able to connect with the natural world around us. Again, let's look at the chakra system to see what we find. The solar plexus chakra's keywords and functions are power, autonomy, metabolism, transformation, self-esteem, will, assertiveness, and the corresponding verb is "I am." The right of the solar plexus is "I have the right to be who I am." The heart chakra's keywords and functions are love, balance, sympathy & empathy, unity, healing, and the corresponding verb and the right of the heart chakra is "I love." The throat chakra's keywords and functions are sound, vibration, communication, mantras, song and the corresponding verb is "I speak." The right of the solar plexus chakra is "I have the right to share and express."

The middle world is everything that is right before you. Here is where we create, put into action, engage, and connect. It is the essence of being alive as a human on earth. Think of the lower world as the roots of the tree. The middle world as the trunk and the upper world as the branches. The trunk is stable and connects and balances the lower aspects with the higher aspects. Without a trunk, the tree would not exist. It is the middle of the tree, here in the middle world.

As described by Abram (1997),

How did Western civilization become so estranged from nonhuman nature, so oblivious to the presence of other animals and the earth, that our current lifestyles and activities contribute daily to the destruction of whole ecosystems—whole forests, river valleys, oceans—and to the extinction of countless species? Or, more specifically, how did civilized humankind lose all sense of reciprocity and relationship with the animate natural world, that rapport that so influences (and limits) the activities of most indigenous, tribal peoples? How did civilization break out of, and leave behind, the animistic or participatory mode of experience known to all native, place-based cultures (p. 135)?

In the book, *The Spell of the Sensuous* Abrams explores the world of the five senses, the phenomenology of experiencing each moment and the meaning of each moment within our five senses. He suggests that humans began to disassociate from the natural (non-human) world when we began to superimpose words which held no meaning into our written language. For example, he takes the reader back in time to a place prior to the English written language. A time when Plato was constructing the Greek alphabet from the Hebrew aleph-beth.

Aleph is the first letter of the Hebrew language, and it means "ox." When we think of an ox, we gain a complete picture within our mind of an animal, an experience, an energetic signature with powerful horns and stability within the world. Yet, we lost the meaning of Aleph as an ox, and simply memorized the letter A to be a symbol without sensation. A is A now vs. A is an ox, can you sense its leadership, strength, and stability. I highly recommend this book to any reader who would like to explore these concepts further. However, for the sake of this book, I will simply say that the Western world has moved away from the heart of the world and into the mind of a human – a separate mind which is disconnected from nature and animals. I am here to say that it hasn't always been this way – and now is time for us to realize that we are connected to everything in a very deep way.

Did you remember the time when we (in human form) are a part of nature (non-human), just as the trees are a part of nature, just as the animals are a part of nature? I invite you into a realm where the physical, emotional, mental and spirit are one. This is a space of the merged, the synthesized expression of all. I invite you to go within – here you will discover your harmony with all of creation, for you are a significant part of the all. Here we are one with everything.

74

I invite you to come with me, as we go on a journey – a journey that is a unique expression of life force. As the universe expresses itself – within each of us, in our own unique vibration – may we receive the wisdom, guidance, and connection that reveals life's greatness within our being and connection to the All.

Imagine that you are standing before a tree, and someone asks you to get to know this tree. There are two very different ways of experiencing and knowing the tree. Personally, I am bi-cognitive, I think in two different cultures and languages. Biologically, I am 50% Navajo and 50% Dutch – hence, I think in both cultures. The thought process here is that the language of any culture is a direct reflection of the cognitive worldview of said culture. The English language speaks in terms of labels or naming things, segregating and separating things in order to break them down into smaller parts in order to understand each part and the whole. Hence, in order to get to know the tree, one would have to segregate and separate the parts and then name the parts in order to know the tree.

For example, the tree has roots, a trunk, branches, and leaves. We will call this one an oak tree. This is very scientifically based and works well, half of the time. However, there is another way of getting to know the tree. The Navajo language describes things and sees things as a part of the whole. One can only know a tree when one experiences a connection to the tree. Hence in order to get to know the tree, one would stand before the tree and notice the complete organism. Next, they would notice that the leaves of a tree are moving in one gentle direction, then they would notice that their own hair is moving in the same direction. At this point, they would connect with the tree and recognize that there is something, a force, that is moving them and the tree in the same motion. This is how they know the tree.

As I ponder this, I recognize that one way is through the lenses of our left hemisphere in our brain, the other is through our right hemisphere in our brain. The left hemisphere is best with understanding language, linear thinking, and logic. The English language seems to be very left hemisphere in nature. The right hemisphere is holistic and intuitive in its processing. The Navajo language seems to be very right hemisphere in nature. I do not favor one over the other, they are complete only with each other. Please do not get stuck in one or the other. There is a beauty between allowing something to be its own individuality yet connecting with it as we know we are all related.

Say not, "I have found the truth," but rather,
"I have found a truth."
Say not, "I have found the path of the soul."
Say rather, "I have met the soul walking upon my path."
For the soul walks upon all paths.
The soul walks not upon a line,
neither does it grow like a reed.
The soul unfolds itself like a lotus of countless petals.
-Kahlil Gibran

IV. The Upper World

The upper world is most aptly described as that which is above us, and that which we grow towards like a tree grows towards the sun. This is a world of higher consciousness. It holds vision and perspective from a higher level.

In accordance with the chakra system presented at the end of chapter one, the upper world can directly correlate to the upper 2.5 chakras - half of the throat chakra, the third-eye chakra, and the crown chakra.

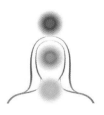

Upper World (Realm)

In order to understand the upper world, we must revisit the keywords and functions of these chakras. Keeping in mind the three main functions of each chakra are as follows: 1) to receive energy, 2) to assimilate energy, and 3) to transmit energy (Judith, 2010).

Again, the throat chakra's keywords and functions are sound, vibration, communication, mantras, song and the corresponding verb is "I speak." The right of the throat chakra is "I have the right to share and express." For example, when the throat chakra is blocked an individual may struggle with express themselves. If unblocked, the throat chakra is able to express one's truth in an influential manner.

The third-eye chakra's keywords and functions are light, seeing, intuition, visualization, perceiving, all the clairs (clairvoyance, clairaudience, etc...), vision, and the corresponding verb and the right is "I see," and "I perceive." For example, when the third-eye chakra is blocked an individual may struggle with trusting their sixth sense and intuition. If unblocked, the third-eye chakra assists us with recognizing our intuition and potentially our sixth-sense gifts.

The crown chakra's keywords and functions are consciousness, thought, information, knowledge, understanding, transcendence, meditation and the corresponding verb and the right of the crown chakra is "I am one with everything." For example, when the crown chakra is blocked an individual may struggle with understanding higher consciousness or esoteric knowledge. If unblocked, the crown chakra is able to connect us with our higher self, guides, and higher consciousness.

The Landscape

There are many landscapes in the upper world. These landscapes can reflect those within the middle world (the physical world in which we physically exist). However, they are not limited to these landscapes. The upper world can appear cosmic, etheric, and have many landscapes that one would not normally experience in the middle world. For example, there might be an experience of traveling through wormholes and visiting other planets. There may be an experience of heavenly halls. There may be an experience of merely floating on clouds. It is limitless.

What beings may one encounter in the upper world? Just like the other worlds, we may encounter middle world type beings such as animals (both mystical and non-mystical), human spirits and otherworldly beings. Additionally, we may encounter angels – it is my understanding that angels love the upper world but are not limited to it. We may encounter ascended masters such as Usui, Buddha, Kwan Yin, etc. We may also encounter loved ones who have passed on to the other side. I have experienced interactions with deities such as gods and goddesses in the upper world. Some may even experience entities which they describe as alien. There is no limit to what one may encounter; which is why it is good to set a solid intention prior to journeying to this (and any) realm.

When journeying to the upper world, it is essential to establish allies within the landscape that will be able to work with you. In the last section of this chapter, there is a guided meditation to the upper world to meet some of these allies if you wish.

The Phenomenon

There are many reasons why someone would want to journey to the upper world – again, it would be nearly impossible to record all of them here in this book. However, I do want to provide a personal and professional example of what can occur.

Historically, I don't like the feeling of being angry – some people do – I am one who finds the sensation of anger to be extremely uncomfortable. As nice as this may make me sound, the truth is that it is perfectly natural to feel anger and it is not healthy to ignore it. Of course, we need to find harmless ways to express our anger; and, it is healthy to honor this energy with respect. However, this is something that I had to learn for myself. So, I was seeking spiritual guidance around anger and my resistance towards anger. Hence, I journeyed to the upper world to meet Sekhmet. Sekhmet (which means "power" or "might") is an Egyptian warrior goddess. She is most often depicted with lioness features – and is referred to as a "powerful one." Hence, I assumed that she would understand anger and even rage – and maybe she could help me.

I found myself on a beach in the upper world. The sky was dark and cloudy. The world seemed a little cold, and the mist coming off of the ocean was chilling me to the core. The waves were crashing hard on the shoreline rocks. It wasn't very peaceful this time – it felt like a storm was brewing.

I called out for Sekhmet a few times, and then I waited to see what would happen. At which point a beautiful large lioness goes running past me and jumps up on a cliff and ROARS!!! Next, she jumps down and runs past me again to another cliff on the other side and lets out another ROAR!!! A few more rounds of this and I was getting a little afraid.

She then comes up to me, looks at me as if to say, "Now it is your turn." Cautiously, I walk up to the ocean and let out a little roar. "Try Again!", she says. I Roar. "Again, this time with everything that you have inside of you!" I take a deep breath, feeling all the stored tension in my being, I let out an earth-shattering ROAR!!! I know it was earth-shattering; because, as I

83

was expressing my stored anger the sky began to crack and fall away into the ocean. The sun came out, and the waves calmed down. The whole landscape changed, my whole world changed. Before I finished this journey, I turned to Sekhmet and said, "Thank you. What can I offer you for showing me how to express myself and hence change my world from storms to clear skies. She replied, "Don't wait so long between visits." And she calmly walked away.

I learned that just because I wasn't expressing my anger, it was still there. It was slowly causing a storm to brew within me. I learned that moving through the energy of anger can be accomplished in a sacred space without harm to anyone. I also recognized that I wasn't angry at a person – I was simply angry at situations. Even though at times I would blame a person for a situation – it is the situation, itself, that made me angry. Next time you experience anger, ask yourself if you are angry at a person or at a situation. It is much easier to allow anger when it is directed at a situation and not a person.

The Hidden Treasures

What are the hidden treasures of the Upper World? What is the purpose of exploring this realm? There are endless reasons why one would travel and explore the upper world, we will begin with what we know thus far from the chakra system.

The throat chakra's keywords and functions are sound, vibration, communication, mantras, song and the corresponding verb is "I speak." The right of the throat chakra is "I have the right to share and express." The third-eye chakra's keywords and functions are light, seeing, intuition, visualization, perceiving, all the clairs (clairvoyance, clairaudience, etc...), vision, and the corresponding verb and the right is "I see, and I perceive." The crown chakra's keywords and functions are consciousness, thought, information, knowledge, understanding, transcendence, meditation and the corresponding verb and the right of the crown chakra is "I am one with everything."

Hence, one would be able to explore the self-actualization aspect. Additionally, one would journey to the upper world in order to connect with and develop our spiritual gifts, connect with our guides, teachers, gods, and goddesses, ascended masters, higher self, angels, and the divine. Think of the upper world like the branches and leaves of a tree. The branches reach up, ever-growing towards the sun in order to draw down vitamins and energy from above. To connect with the heavens and create a photosynthesis effect and assist the world that it is connected with, sharing life, etc. Hence, these are the aspects that one would find in the upper world.

For example, I have traveled to the upper world to assist in gaining esoteric wisdom, answers, lessons from a higher consciousness, or to gain a higher understanding of connecting with the All. As with the other worlds, there are countless situations that one could journey to the upper world for; however, it is essential to state one's intention prior to embarking on a journey. Additionally, you may want to seek out an individual (Shamanic Practitioner) to assist your journey or journey on your behalf. Safety is key!

This being said, I have created a guided meditation for you that will be safe and easy so that you will be able to experience the upper world in a sacred guided spiritual way. Below you can read about it, and you can also find this guided meditation on the Granddaughter Crow YouTube channel if you'd like to experience it without interruptions. Or find a friend with a calm voice to read this to you (take turns, it's fun).

First, place yourself in a comfortable place that you feel safe and will not be disturbed. Now, sit or lay in a relaxing manner. Next, begin to breathe with the three-fold breath that is mentioned earlier in the book. Breathe like this for at least a minute, more if you'd like. Next, do a body scan and check in with your body to see if there is any part of you that would like to shift and/or relax more. Please feel free to relax.

If you need to shift your body at any time during this meditation, it will not disturb the meditation. Please feel the comfort of this sacred space. Now, let's continue... visualize that you are in a comfortable sphere. Within this sphere is scared space, visualize a beautiful, yet peaceful light filling up this sphere with sacred loving energy. Now, as you breathe in, know that you are breathing in sacred energy. As you hold it within your being, know that you are holding sacred energy within your being. As you exhale, know that you are releasing and relaxing into sacred space. We are ready.

We are at the top of five steps. Let's descend these steps together. Five, relax, four, relax, three, relax, two, relax, one. Now we find ourselves in a small yet cozy room where there is a table, a coat rack, and a door. First, let's move over to the table. I invite you to set down anything and everything that you are carrying and place it on this table. There is a sign from the Universe above the table, and it reads, "Anything that you set here, will be taken care of."

Next, let's move over to the coat rack where we can hang up the many hats and cloaks that we wear in our daily lives. Next, prepare yourself, as we are going to move over to the door. Beyond this door is a beautiful land. When you are ready, open the door, step through the door, and allow the door to gently close behind you.

You have entered a beautiful meadow. Listen carefully, for there is the sound of large wings on the horizon. As you shift your eyes, you begin to see a horse with wings coming out of the air and landing before you where you stand. This horse is beautiful, strong and full of love and protection. This is your ally companion and guide on this journey. As this beautiful creature stands before you, you feel that it is asking you to climb up and sit upon its back. So, you gently mount the horse, make yourself comfortable and hold on. When this magickal horse realizes that you are ready to go, it begins to move forward to a gallop and begins to ascend into the air, leaving the ground below.

Higher and higher you ascend into the sky. Up, up, up to the clouds. You can sense the clouds around you. As you continue to ascend, you find yourself on top of the clouds, moving on them as though they were now the earth below.

In the distance, you see a landscape. It slowly begins to focus into sight. It is beautiful and plush. The horse gently lands into the landscape, slowing coming to a halt and you dismount. The horse waits there for you as you begin to look around. Call out from your being to any guide or holy divine teacher. Wait for them, and they will appear to you. Share with them and listen to what they wish to share with you.

Take your time. (Pause here for at least 3 minutes).

When you are finished, ask them what they would like for you to give them. Allow them to give you a gift, as well. Thank your guide for their guidance and gift.

When you are ready, find your way back to the magickal horse. Mount the horse and the horse gently lifts off and returns you through the clouds and safely back to the meadow. Thank the horse for sharing this time with you and find the door, open the door, walk through the door and allow the door to gently close behind you. Move over to the stairs, and we will ascend these five steps gently as you re-enter this room. One, two, three, four, five. You are safely back in this room. Take your time, wiggle your fingers and toes. When you are ready, gently open your eyes.

At this point, I would like to invite you to either write down or discuss with a trusted friend what you encountered. Who did you encounter? What did they share with you? What did you share with them? What gift did you give them? What gift did they give you? Just like waking from a dream, it is time to sit with the experience and allow the meaning to unfold. What hidden treasure did you find in the upper world?

V. The Destination

It is said that it is not about the destination, it is about the journey. I agree. However, if the destination is a state of existence such as happiness, freedom, harmony, I believe that most of us are innately moving to these states. The journey to such states can be full of initiations, as presented in the first chapter. In this sense, I believe that the outcome of initiations is the rite of passage to carry medicine (wisdom). This wisdom can be a cornerstone which we live by, and it can be shared with the world around us to assist others in finding their state of balance and harmony. Additionally, I believe that the process of initiations holds three main stages. The three main stages are as follows: 1) life, 2) death, and 3) rebirth.

Life is the active state of growing, sustaining, and experiencing in an active way. Death is a letting go and moving forward, a release of the old. Rebirth is the new state in which we begin to experience the world around us from a refreshed point-of-view, a new perspective. Although we can see this process in all of its stages in the physical body, it can and does happen on an emotional, mental and spiritual state, as well.

Hence, initiations can be emotional. It is a letting go of an old emotion that no longer suits us at this point in the journey. For example, maybe it no longer serves us to experience and feel certain emotions; so, we allow them to flow away and step into new emotions. An old emotion might be saying that we are less than others or broken, a new emotion would be for us to realize that we are perfectly authentic just like everyone else. A life example of this might be a breakup with an old partner that assisted you with feeling less than. There was a life with this old partner, then a death when we let go, then rebirth as we experience new emotional states.

Initiations can be on a mental level. It can be a letting go of an old idea about self or others that no longer serve us at this point on our path. For example, an individual who did not perform well academically in high school may think that they are not intelligent enough; however, the same individual may thrive in college. Hence, the thought and idea of lacking enough intellect needs to die, and the new idea of becoming more intelligent needs to be born and can be fed. This process sounds easy, but it is not. It can come with challenges and the need for courage to give yourself a shot.

Initiations can happen on a spiritual level, as well. These can come in a multitude of different ways. They can come as a burst, or as a vision quest, or through the process of life. With this one, I believe it is most important to ask questions to gain and grow.

There is an ancient Navajo teaching that reveals the purpose in life. It is said that the purpose in life is to continuously grow in our four bodies of existence – to seek balance as we grow. As simple as this may sound, growth and balance occur in countless ways.

The sacred clockwise spiral speaks to us of continuous growth.

It is said that we entered this physical body through the sacred spiral at the crown of our head. It is said that the spiral fingerprints on the tips of our fingers are sacred. Hence, what we do is sacred.

The journey of the soul and the wisdom of the medicine person is open to any individual who is willing to take this adventure. It is not limited but ever expanding.

We earn the medicine that we carry. We earn the wisdom. We earn the rite of passage. We earn these things and more through life's initiations - the difficult times. Once we move through an initiation, we have the opportunity to extract the greatest wisdom and carry the wisdom with us – as medicine people.

Please join me on the journey of the soul.

Let's make it an adventure!

References

Abram, D. (1997). *The spell of the sensuous*. New

    York, NY: Vintage Books.

Andrews, T. (2003). *Animal speaks*. St. Paul, MN:

    Llewellyn Publications.

Buhner, S. H. (2004). *The secret teachings of plants*.

    Rochester, VT: Bear & Company.

Gardner, H. E. (2008). *Multiple intelligences: New*

    horizons in theory and practice. Basic Books.

Gibran, K. (1923). *The prophet*. New York, NY: Alfred

    A. Knoff, Inc.

Judith, A. (2010). *Wheel of life* (2nd ed.). Woodbury,

    MN: Llewellyn Worldwide.

Moustakas, C. E. (1994). *Phenomenological research methods*. Thousand Oaks, CA: Sage Publications.

Simpson, L. (1999). *The book of chakra healing*. New Your, NY: Sterling.

van Manen, M. (2002). *Writing in the dark*. Ontario, Canada: The Althouse Press.

About the Author

Dr. Joy "Granddaughter Crow" Gray Bio:

"I am here to serve, inspire, and encourage."
Dr. Joy "Granddaughter Crow" Gray has received a BSBM/BSBA, MBA, and a Doctorate in Leadership. With several years' experience in Corporate America with an International Company, additional time working with the Government, as well as, a College Professor - she is here to share and serve under the name of Granddaughter Crow.

Internationally recognized as a Medicine Women, Dr. Joy "Granddaughter Crow" Gray was born an Empath and Medium comes from a long lineage of spiritual leaders and esoteric wisdom. Raised by spiritual leaders, as a child, she was fashioned and trained to serve the people through ministry. Member of the Navajo Nation (50%) and Dutch Heritage (50%) – she is able to provide a sense of integration through life experience.

Inducted into Delta Mu Delta, International Honors Society in 2012. Voted in as Women of the Year 2015, by the NAPW (National Association of Professional Women). Featured in Native Max Magazine June/July 2016 issue.

In 2014, founded The Eagle Heart Foundation. A 501(c)(3) nonprofit organization dedicated to charitable giving and educational enhancement of the Native American population for the purpose of honoring the ancestors and responding to their heartfelt prayers.

Websites:

www.granddaughtercrow.com

www.eagleheartfoundation.com